I CAN I WILL

I CAN I WILL

DECLARATIONS FOR YOUTH

Copyright © 2023 by Robin Totten

All rights reserved. This book or any portion thereof may not be reproduced or used in any manner whatsoever without the express written permission of the publisher except for the use of brief quotations in a book review.

ISBN: Hardcover 979-8-218-14495-1

Bible verses from New International Version {NIV}and the New Living Translation {NLT}

Design and publishing assistance by The Happy Self-Publisher.

Dedication

For every child who wants to be good and do good.
And for Ruke, the kindest kid I know.

Introduction

Simple Instructions and Promises in God's Word

Proverbs 20:11 says, Even children are known by the way they act, whether their conduct is pure, and whether it is right (NLT).

A relationship with God is needed for pure, right conduct. God's word says we are to teach His laws to our children and their children. Every generation has that command and expectation. The declarations in this book are one way for you to begin your learning and your relationship. If you already have a relationship with God, my hope is that this book will encourage and inspire you to keep growing in knowledge and discipline as you commit to know God more.

In its most basic, simplistic form, God's word consists of two main parts: instructions and promises. It is my intention and my hope that you will gain a better understanding of both after engaging with this book.

Peter 1:5-8 says, In view of all this, make every effort to respond to God's promises. Supplement your faith with a generous provision of moral excellence, and moral excellence with knowledge, and knowledge with self-control, and self-control with patient endurance, and patient endurance with godliness, and godliness with brotherly affection, and brotherly affection with love for everyone. The more you grow like this, the more productive and useful you will be in your knowledge of our Lord Jesus Christ. (NLT)

You are beginning a study in God's word that will give you positive affirmations, His instructions and His promises to you.

       Enjoy,
       Robin

Suggestions For Use

Each two-word, alliterative declaration can be read aloud, proceeded by the phrase, "I can I will."

Focus on learning and understanding one declaration a day. Try to demonstrate that declaration in your daily life. Put it into practice.

Make it personal. Research and write another related verse. What comes to mind when you read the verse?

In the space provided on each page, write about what each declaration means to you. One way to do this is to rewrite the verse in your own words.

Think about how you might apply the declaration in your day.

Own it. Read the verses in other Bible translations to solidify your understanding (both New Living Translation (NLT), and New International Version (NIV) are used in this book).

I CAN I WILL
Answer Accurately

Colossians 4:6 Let your conversation be always full of grace, seasoned with salt, so that you may know how to answer everyone. (NIV)

Peter 3:15 But in your hearts revere Christ as Lord. Always be prepared to give an answer to everyone who asks you to give the reason for the hope that you have. But do this with gentleness and respect. (NIV)

What these verses mean to me   OR   How I can apply these verses

I CAN I WILL

Be Bold

Joshua 1:9 Have I not commanded you? Be strong and courageous. Do not be afraid; do not be discouraged, for the Lord your God will be with you wherever you go. (NIV)

Acts 4:29 And now, O Lord, hear their threats, and give us, your servants, great boldness in preaching your word. (NLT)

What these verses mean to me   OR   How I can apply these verses

I CAN I WILL

Completely Commit

Psalm 37:5 Commit your way to the Lord; trust in Him and He will do this. (NIV)

Luke 9:62 Jesus replied, No one who puts a hand to the plow and looks back is fit for service in the kingdom of God. (NIV)

What these verses mean to me   OR   How I can apply these verses

I CAN I WILL

Defeat Doubt

James 1:6 When you ask, be sure that your faith is in God alone. Do not waiver, for a person with divided loyalty is unsettled as a wave of the sea that is blown and tossed by the wind. (NLT).

Psalm 94:19 When doubts filled my mind, Your comfort gave me renewed hope and cheer. (NLT)

What these verses mean to me   OR   How I can apply these verses

I CAN I WILL
Enjoy Everything

Ecclesiastes 2:24 A person can do nothing better than to eat and drink and find satisfaction in their own toil. This too, I see, is from the hand of God. (NIV).

John 17:13 Now I am coming to you. I told them many things while I was with them in this world so they would be filled with my joy. (NLT)

What these verses mean to me   OR   How I can apply these verses

I CAN I WILL

Forget Fear

Psalm 46:2 Therefore we will not fear, though the earth give way and the mountains fall into the heart of the sea. (NIV)

Timothy 1:7 For God has not given us a spirit of fear and timidity, but of power, love, and self-discipline. (NLT)

What these verses mean to me   OR   How I can apply these verses

I CAN I WILL
Give Generously

Deuteronomy 15:10 Give generously to them and do so without a grudging heart; then because of this the Lord your God will bless you in all your work and in everything you put your hand to. (NIV)

Luke 6:38 Give, and you will receive. Your gift will return to you in full pressed down, shaken together to make room for more, running over, and poured into your lap. The amount you give will determine the amount you get back. (NLT).

What these verses mean to me   OR   How I can apply these verses

I CAN I WILL

Honor Home

Psalms 101:2 I will be careful to live a blameless life - when will you come to help me? I will lead a life of integrity in my own home. (NLT)

Proverbs 14:1 The wise woman builds her house, but with her own hands the foolish one tears hers down. (NIV)

What these verses mean to me   OR   How I can apply these verses

I CAN I WILL
Ignore Impossible

Genesis 18:14 Is anything too hard for the Lord? I will return about this time next year, and Sarah will have a son. (NLT)

Luke 1:37 For no word from God will ever fail. (NIV)

What these verses mean to me   OR   How I can apply these verses

I CAN I WILL

Join Jesus

John 14:12 Very truly I tell you, anyone who believes in me will do the same works I have done, and even greater works because I am going to be with the Father. (NLT)

Philippians 3:10 I want to know Christ—yes, to know the power of his resurrection and participation in his sufferings, becoming like him in his death. (NIV)

What these verses mean to me   OR   How I can apply these verses

I CAN I WILL
Keep Knowledge

Proverbs 18:15 Intelligent people are always ready to learn. Their ears are open to knowledge. (NLT)

Timothy 3:14 But you must remain faithful to the things you have been taught. You know they are true, for you know you can trust those who taught you. (NLT)

What these verses mean to me   OR   How I can apply these verses

I CAN I WILL

Love Loud

John 13:34 So now I am giving you a new commandment: Love each other. Just as I have loved you, you should love each other. (NLT)

Romans 13:10 Love does no harm to a neighbor. Therefore love is the fulfillment of the law. (NIV)

What these verses mean to me   OR   How I can apply these verses

I CAN I WILL

Master Money

Matthew 6:24 No one can serve two masters. For you will hate one and love the other; you will be devoted to one and despise the other. You cannot serve God and be enslaved to money. (NLT)

Timothy 6:17 Teach those who are rich in this world not to be proud and not to trust in their money, which is so unreliable. Their trust should be in God, who richly gives us all we need for our enjoyment. (NLT)

What these verses mean to me   OR   How I can apply these verses

I CAN I WILL
Notice Names

Exodus 3:15 God also said to Moses, "Say this to the Israelites, The Lord, the God of your fathers-the God of Abraham, the God of Isaac and the God of Jacob-has sent me to you." This is my name forever, the name you shall call me from generation to generation. (NIV)

Exodus 33:17 The Lord replied to Moses, "I will indeed do what you have asked, for I look favorably on you, and I know you by name." (NLT)

What these verses mean to me   OR   How I can apply these verses

I CAN I WILL
Overcome Offense

Proverbs 10:12 Hatred stirs up quarrels, but love makes up for all offenses. (NLT)

Matthew 18:15 If another believer sins against you, go privately and point out the offense. If the other person listens and confesses it, you have won that person back. (NLT)

What these verses mean to me   OR   How I can apply these verses

I CAN I WILL
Practice Peace

John 14:27 I am leaving you with a gift—peace of mind and heart. And the peace I give is a gift the world cannot give. So don't be troubled or afraid. (NLT)

Romans 12:18 If it is possible, as far as it depends on you, live at peace with everyone. (NIV)

What these verses mean to me   OR   How I can apply these verses

I CAN I WILL
Quit Quarreling

Timothy 2:23 Again I say, don't get involved in foolish, ignorant arguments that only start fights. (NLT)

Philippians 2:14 Do everything without grumbling or arguing. (NIV)

What these verses mean to me   OR   How I can apply these verses

I CAN I WILL
Remember Rules

Matthew 7:12 Do to others whatever you would have them to do to you. This is the essence of all that is taught in the law and the prophets. (NLT)

Proverbs 4:14 Do not set foot on the path of the wicked or walk on the way of evildoers. (NIV)

What these verses mean to me   OR   How I can apply these verses

I CAN I WILL
Seek Support

Proverbs 24:6 Surely you need guidance to wage war, and victory is won through many advisers. (NIV)

Ecclesiastes 4:9 Two people are better off than one, for they can help each other succeed. (NLT)

What these verses mean to me   OR   How I can apply these verses

I CAN I WILL
Tell Truth

Zechariah 8:16 But this is what you must do: Tell the truth to each other. Render verdicts in your courts that are just and that lead to peace. (NIV)

Colossians 3:9 Don't lie to each other, for you have stripped off your old sinful nature and all its wicked deeds. (NLT)

What these verses mean to me   OR   How I can apply these verses

I CAN I WILL

Use Uniqueness

Corinthians 12:4 There are different kinds of spiritual gifts, but the same Spirit is the source of them all. (NLT)

Peter 4:10 Each of you should use whatever gift you have received to serve others, as faithful stewards of God's grace in its various forms. (NIV)

What these verses mean to me   OR   How I can apply these verses

I CAN I WILL

Value Vows

Numbers 30:2 A man who makes a vow to the Lord or makes a pledge under oath must never break it. He must do exactly what he said he would do. (NLT)

Ecclesiastes 5:4 When you make a promise to God, don't delay in following through, for God takes no pleasure in fools. Keep all the promises you make to him. (NLT)

What these verses mean to me   OR   How I can apply these verses

I CAN I WILL

Wage War

Corinthians 16:13 Be on guard. Stand firm in the faith. Be courageous. Be strong. (NIV)

Ephesians 6:13 Therefore, put on every piece of God's armor so you will be able to resist the enemy in the time of evil. Then after the battle you will still be standing firm. (NLT)

What these verses mean to me   OR   How I can apply these verses

I CAN I WILL
eXhalt eXcellence

Daniel 6:3 Daniel soon proved himself more capable than all the other administrators and high officers. Because of Daniel's great ability, the king made plans to place him over the entire empire. (NLT)

Proverbs 22:29 Do you see someone skilled in their work? They will serve before kings; they will not serve before officials of low rank. (NIV)

What these verses mean to me   OR   How I can apply these verses

I CAN I WILL

Yield Young

Lamentations 3:27 And it is good for a man to bear the yoke while he is young. (NIV)

Matthew 18:3 Then He said, I tell you the truth, unless you turn from your sins and become like little children, you will never get into the Kingdom of Heaven. (NLT)

What these verses mean to me   OR   How I can apply these verses

I CAN I WILL

Zest Zeal

Romans 12:11 Never be lazy but work hard and serve the Lord enthusiastically. (NLT)

Acts 18:25 He had been instructed in the way of the Lord, and he spoke with great fervor and taught about Jesus accurately, though he knew only the baptism of John. (NIV)

What these verses mean to me   OR   How I can apply these verses

About the Author

Robin Totten is a retired special needs teacher living in Middletown, Delaware.

She is the author of *Words Breathe,* a book of prose. *I Can I Will* is her second work. It is designed specifically for young people wanting to develop their faith and strengthen their relationship with God.